Blues
Legends

by Stephanie Wilder

Scott Foresman
is an imprint of

Glenview, Illinois • Boston, Massachusetts • Chandler, Arizona
Upper Saddle River, New Jersey

A scene from the American South, where the blues was invented

The Roots of the Blues

Much of African American history is filled with sadness. That sadness, however, is often mingled with hope for the future. These two emotions, sadness and hope, are at the heart of the great American musical tradition of the blues.

The United States' enslaved African Americans were freed in 1865. Before then **slavery** existed throughout the American South. For more than a hundred years African Americans had been made to work without pay. They were free to do only what they were told.

The end of slavery did little to improve African Americans' lives. Most remained poor, and what work they could find didn't pay enough. A special set of laws known as Jim Crow laws were written to keep African Americans from having many of the rights that other Americans had.

The blues were inspired partly by the songs sung by sharecroppers.

Taking Strength from Music

When slavery ended, many African Americans became sharecroppers, or farmers who rent their land from others. While laboring in the fields, they often sang songs to pass the time. These songs had their roots in the songs of the enslaved. And those songs had roots in the music of Africa.

African music didn't originally have the blues' sad and mournful feel. But the music changed to reflect the hardships African Americans faced. African Americans also sang hopeful songs, such as the spirituals they sang when they met together in church. Eventually these two types of songs came together to form the blues.

The blues first became popular with sharecroppers in the lower South. Soon everyone was playing or listening to the blues, from the local **barber** to national audiences. White listeners also embraced the new style of music, and in the 1950s, musicians combined it with country music to create rock 'n' roll. Almost every kind of popular music played in the United States today is based partly on the blues. But it all started with just a handful of African American musicians. This book will tell their story.

Ma Rainey: Mother of the Blues

On April 26, 1886, Gertrude Pridgett was born in Columbus, Georgia. She began performing at the age of fourteen when she participated in a local talent show. A few years later, while in St. Louis, she heard some music that was totally new to her. What she heard was an early form of the blues. Ms. Pridgett was greatly influenced by the music and made it the focus of her singing.

In 1904 she married William "Pa" Rainey. From that point on she was known simply as Ma Rainey. She traveled and performed with her husband all over the South. Ma Rainey is known as the first female blues singer. Her nickname is "Mother of the Blues."

Ma Rainey was named "Mother of the Blues" for having been one of the first female blues singers.

Ma Rainey had a powerful voice that brought meaning and emotion to her songs. Although primarily a singer of rough, country-style blues songs, she also added some polished, city-style blues to her singing.

During the 1900s men usually sang in the country style and women in the city style. Ma Rainey mixed the sounds and themes of both styles. She gained respect for writing her own songs and made things easier for other female blues singers by proving that women could sing the blues.

Ma Rainey's Recordings

During the early 1900s Ma Rainey traveled with a group called Tolliver's Circus and Musical Extravaganza. Ma's voice and singing became known and liked by more and more people as the group toured around the country. However, Ma Rainey's fans were limited at first to those who saw her live performances. This is because she had to wait many years to record any of her music.

In 1923 Ma Rainey finally **released** her first phonograph recording. This meant that people could listen to and enjoy her music at home on a phonograph, or record player, a machine that was used before the invention of tape and compact disc players. They no longer had to travel to a live performance to hear her.

Ma Rainey's recordings sold well. In response, she recorded ninety-two songs over the next five years.

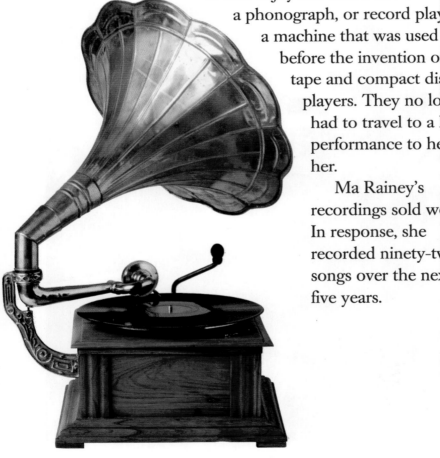

People played Ma Rainey's records on phonographs such as this.

Ma Rainey's music often dealt with problems facing African Americans. Her song "Slave to the Blues" makes references to slavery. Ma Rainey's songs also made references to the Jim Crow laws that Southern states enforced at the time. These laws took away many of the freedoms that African Americans thought they would gain when slavery ended.

Ma Rainey's music contained a powerful message. She sang about things that her African American audience could relate to. With her strong voice and passionate lyrics, Ma Rainey helped the blues become more popular.

Phonograph players became less popular during the 1980s, as people began listening to music recorded on cassette tapes (left) and compact discs (upper left).

Bessie Smith: Empress of the Blues

Bessie Smith was born in Chattanooga, Tennessee, sometime around 1894. Her childhood was a hard one. Smith's parents died when she was very young. Bessie and her brothers and sisters were poor and had to depend on each other. Her older sister Viola raised her, and her brother Clarence taught her to sing and dance.

Around 1912 Clarence got Bessie an audition as a dancer with Moses Stokes' traveling show. Bessie won the job and began performing on the road. While traveling she met Ma Rainey, who would have a great influence on her career.

Bessie Smith (left) was influenced by Ma Rainey's singing and style of music.

Ma Rainey took Bessie, who was still very young at the time, under her wing. She became Bessie's mentor, sharing what she knew about singing and the blues.

Smith's singing career took off while she was under Ma Rainey's guidance. She added many of Ma Rainey's techniques to her music, while at the same time developing her own unique style of singing.

With training and practice, Smith became a great blues singer. Throughout the 1920s she traveled the South and sang to sold-out crowds. She earned more than a thousand dollars a week for her performances, which easily would have made her a millionaire in today's money.

Bessie Smith, who started as a dancer, would eventually find fame as a blues singer.

Bessie Smith enjoyed great success during the 1920s, only to experience a decline in the 1930s as swing music became more popular.

In 1923, the same year that Ma Rainey put out her first phonograph recordings, Bessie Smith also began making records. One of her first, called "Downhearted Blues," sold more than 700,000 copies in only six months! Bessie recorded 160 songs in ten years and became known as the "Empress of the Blues." Both city and country listeners enjoyed Smith's music, which blended Ma Rainey's far more country-music singing style with lyrics and a sound that city audiences found appealing.

Sadly, Bessie's career went into decline during the 1930s. Much of this was due to the Great Depression. The Great Depression caused millions of Americans to lose their jobs. People wanted their music to be more upbeat during this grim time, so swing music, which was more optimistic than the blues, became more popular. People also had far less money to spend on records and concert tickets, which also hurt Bessie's career.

Despite these problems, Bessie Smith performed throughout the 1930s until her death in 1937. She is remembered today as one of the most successful blues singers of the 1920s.

Ray Charles:
The Father of Soul

Ray Charles, "The Father of Soul," was born Ray Charles Robinson in Albany, Georgia, on September 23, 1930. He began playing the piano as a very young child, giving his first public performance in a Florida café at the age of five.

Ray had a difficult childhood. He grew up during the worst of the Great Depression, and his family had very little money. At the age of six, Ray began losing his sight and became completely blind by age seven.

On top of this, Ray, like Bessie Smith, had to deal with the early deaths of his parents. Ray's father died when Ray was only ten. His mother died when he was just fifteen. Somehow Ray found a way to overcome these hardships and developed into a great blues artist.

Ray's family moved to Florida when he was an infant. There Ray attended a special school called the St. Augustine School for the Deaf and Blind. While at school in Saint Augustine, Ray continued to play the piano. He also learned to play the saxophone and clarinet. Early on, Ray's teachers noticed that he had a gift for music. They also saw that he compensated for his lack of sight by learning how to listen with great care, a skill that helped him greatly to understand the music that he heard.

Ray left school at age fifteen to begin a career as a professional musician. Almost immediately he began developing a unique style of music. Ray spent the late 1940s performing around the country with different blues bands. During the 1950s he continued to perform throughout the United States.

Ray Charles learned how to play many instruments, but he is most remembered as a piano player.

Ray's New Sound

People called Ray's new style of music soul. Soul combined the blues, jazz, gospel, and country, and audiences loved it.

Ray enjoyed a string of hit songs in the 1950s, starting with 1951's "Baby Let Me Hold Your Hand." His song "Things That I Used to Do" sold a million copies in 1954. In that same year, Ray recorded the song "I've Got a Woman," which got him an even bigger following.

By 1959, with the release of "What'd I Say," Ray Charles had become an international pop star. At that time, few African American artists had been able to "cross over," or have success with white audiences. But everyone, regardless of color, wanted to hear Ray's music.

As the years went by Ray traveled less but recorded more. His 1962 album *More Sounds in Country and Western Music* sold more than one million copies. In 1986 Ray Charles was inducted into the Rock and Roll Hall of Fame. He was presented with the National Medal of Arts in 1992 for his achievements in popular music. Ray Charles died on June 10, 2004.

Ray Charles sold millions of records over his career, which spanned almost seven decades.

Aretha Franklin: The Queen of Soul

Aretha Franklin is another famous soul singer. Her music has earned her the title "Queen of Soul."

Franklin was born on March 25, 1942, in Memphis, Tennessee. She grew up in Detroit, Michigan, where her father was a church minister.

Aretha Franklin honed her amazing voice singing gospel music in her father's church.

As a child and young **teenager**, Aretha Franklin sang gospel music in her father's church **choir**. She came to **appreciate** gospel for its power and beauty, and it would influence the rest of her singing career.

Aretha's father had a national radio show and was an important figure in African American culture. He was able to introduce Aretha to several important gospel singers who helped guide her young career. In 1956 she recorded her first album, *The Gospel Sound of Aretha Franklin*.

Aretha moved to New York at the age of eighteen. There she began performing live at both clubs and concert halls, singing for primarily African American audiences.

In 1966 Aretha's career took off. She recorded a series of hits, including "I Never Loved a Man (the Way I Loved You)," "Chain of Fools," "Dr. Feelgood," "Baby, I Love You," and "Respect."

Of all these hits, "Respect" had a unique status. Leaders in both the feminist and African American civil rights movements embraced "Respect" for the way it seemed to symbolize women's and African Americans' struggle for equal rights.

Aretha Franklin performing in Atlantic City, New Jersey in 1989

Aretha Franklin continued to record major hits during the 1970s, including "Spanish Harlem," "Bridge Over Troubled Water," and "Daydreaming." In 1977 she sang at President Jimmy Carter's inauguration. Then, in 1980, Aretha appeared in the hit comedy movie *The Blues Brothers*, which also starred Ray Charles and other notable blues artists. The movie made Aretha popular with a whole new generation of fans and helped revive her career.

In 1985 Aretha won a Grammy award for her hit song "Freeway of Love." It was Aretha's first Grammy award in a decade and showed that she could still produce hits a quarter-century after her first recordings. In 1987 Aretha was inducted into the Rock and Roll Hall of Fame, becoming the first female artist to earn that honor.

Aretha Franklin's most recent albums have focused mostly on her roots in gospel and **religious** singing. Aretha continues to earn respect as a legendary singer of the blues.

A shot of Memphis's Beale Street, famed for its blues music

Back to Where It All Began

The first blues music was played in the American South during the early 1900s. The blues was a product of major cities, such as Atlanta and St. Louis. It also sprang up from the countryside in places such as the Mississippi delta.

The blues had its roots in both African culture and American slavery. Even so, it was a new form of music. It had a sound and style that was uniquely American. African American singers, such as Ma Rainey and Bessie Smith, made the music popular during the 1920s. They sang about their experiences as African Americans in ways that touched the lives of their listeners. Their powerful music helped many people work through the challenges in their lives.

Segregation and slavery no longer exist in the United States, but blues music lives on. Modern legends, including Ray Charles and Aretha Franklin, created music that owed much to the blues. They took the early blues sound and mixed it with other musical styles to create soul music, which reached an even wider audience. Thanks to these musical legends, blues music remains popular today and continues to inspire many talented musicians.

Glossary

appreciate *v.* to think highly of; to recognize the worth or value of

barber *n.* a person whose business is cutting hair and shaving or trimming beards

choir *n.* a group of singers who sing together, often at a church service

released *v.* permitted to be published or sold

religious *adj.* interested in the belief, study, and worship of God or gods

slavery *n.* the practice of holding people against their will and making them work without pay

teenager *n.* a person between the ages of thirteen and nineteen